USBORNE HOTSHOTS
BIRDWATCHING

USBORNE HOTSHOTS
BIRDWATCHING

Edited by Felicity Brooks
Designed by Fiona Johnson

Illustrated by Trevor Boyer,
Ian Jackson and Chris Shields

Consultant: Peter Holden

Series editor: Judy Tatchell
Series designer: Ruth Russell

CONTENTS

How to use this book

This book shows many of the birds of Britain and Ireland and helps you to identify them. Most are found in other parts of Europe as well. Some are common types, or species, that you may see near your home. Others are rarer. How many can you spot and record on the scorecard on pages 30-31?

The measurements in this book show how long a bird would be if it were stretched out like this. The pictures are not shown to scale.

Kingfisher | 17cm |

The parts of a bird

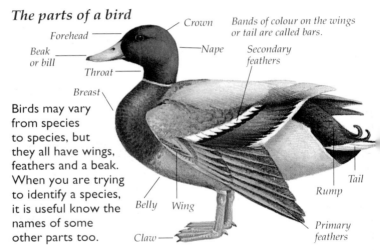

Crown

Bands of colour on the wings or tail are called bars.

Forehead

Nape

Beak or bill

Secondary feathers

Throat

Breast

Birds may vary from species to species, but they all have wings, feathers and a beak. When you are trying to identify a species, it is useful know the names of some other parts too.

Belly   Wing

Claw

Tail

Rump

Primary feathers

Notes and sketches

Quick notes and sketches will help you to remember what you see when you are birdwatching. Your sketches can start with two ovals for the bird's head and body. They do not have to be life-like.

Where to spot birds

Birds are almost everywhere. You can watch them from a window or in a park or garden. Forests, rivers, lakes, seashores and open country are good places to spot birds.

A bird feeder, such as this half coconut, will attract Blue Tits and other acrobatic birds.

What to look for

When trying to identify a bird, ask yourself these questions: What size and shape is it? What colour is it? Does it have any special markings? What shape is its beak? Where does it live? How does it feed?

Sometimes the males and females of a species look different from each other.

Ptarmigan in summer

Ptarmigan in winter

Mallards

Duck (female)

Drake (male)

A bird may have different plumages (feathers) in summer and winter.

The young birds (juveniles) of a species may look different from the adults.

Adult Cuckoo

Juvenile Cuckoo

Seasonal changes

The species of birds you can see in your area will vary with the seasons. Some species move from one place to another for the winter. Others stay in one area all year. Spring is a good time for watching birds, as there are plenty around and they are busy nesting and raising young.

In spring, birds start singing early in the morning.

Blackbird

5

Birds in the garden

Even small gardens are visited by a variety of birds all year round. You can attract more birds to a garden by putting out food and water, especially in winter.

Greenfinches are frequent visitors to gardens, especially in the winter.

Bullfinches

Female

Male

| 15cm |

The white rump shows in flight.

Bullfinches may be found in garden hedges. They eat seeds but also feed on the buds of fruit trees and bushes.

Greenfinches

| 15cm |

Female

Male

The Dunnock, once called the Hedge Sparrow, is a garden bird often seen near bushes.

Dunnock

| 14.5cm |

Blue Tits and Great Tits can often be seen hanging almost upside-down from twigs and bird feeders.

Blue wings

Blue Tit

| 11cm |

Black head

Great Tit

| 14cm |

Broad black band on breast

Great Tits live in woods and gardens and are the largest European tits. They nest in tree holes or nestboxes.

Hanging feeders

Great Tits

Hanging bird feeders filled with peanuts will attract small, acrobatic birds to your garden.

The Wren is a tiny, active bird which is very common and easy to recognize. It often creeps about in dense undergrowth in search of insects and spiders.

Pale stripe over eye

Wren

9.5cm

The tail is often held up.

Spotted Flycatcher

14cm

The Spotted Flycatcher may be seen in gardens in summer. It catches insects in flight and nests in ivy on walls or against tree trunks.

Green Woodpecker

32cm

Green Woodpeckers* visit large gardens and look for ants on the ground. They are about the size of pigeons.

Collared Doves

30cm

Thin, black half-collar

White on tail

Collared Doves are often found in large gardens, parks or around farm buildings. They are sometimes seen in flocks.

Goldfinches feeds on plant seeds in open places, and they particularly like thistles and teasels. They nest in trees.

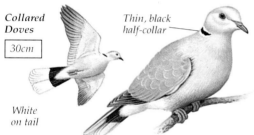

Goldfinches

12cm

Yellow wing bar

*Green Woodpeckers are rare in Scotland, and no Woodpeckers are found in Ireland.

More garden visitors

Blackbirds are common garden birds in Europe. When feeding, they stand with their heads to one side, listening for worms. Young birds have spottier plumages than females.

Robin

Female

Male

Blackbirds

25cm

Bright red breast

14cm

Robins are familiar visitors to gardens and are easy to identify. They sing almost all year. Males and females look the same.

Redwings

Reddish underwing

Magpie

21cm

Redwings visit gardens in cold weather. They may be seen feeding on berries or hunting for worms.

Look for white wing patches.

46cm

Fieldfare

25.5cm

The Fieldfare is recognizable by its blue-grey head and rump, but at a distance it may look like a Mistle Thrush (see page 9).

Magpies are found in both town and country and are easy to spot. They may be seen in flocks in the winter and eat eggs and young birds in spring.

8

Chaffinches

15cm

Female

Male

Chaffinches feed on the ground and eat mainly seeds. They often flock with other finches in winter.

Wagtails hunt insects on lawns. White Wagtails are widespread in Europe, but only the Pied nests in Britain.

Pied Wagtail

White Wagtail

Both species wag their tails up and down.

18cm

Song Thrushes

23cm

Song Thrushes are often seen in or near trees or bushes. In summer they eat lots of snails.

Orange-brown under wing

Mistle Thrushes

White under wing

Mistle Thrushes are a little bigger than Song Thrushes and have larger spots on their breasts. They are sometimes seen in large gardens.

27cm

Collecting feathers

Since most birds change their feathers every year, discarded feathers are not hard to find. Keep any you collect in a notebook.

Make two slits 0.5cm apart. Thread the feather through and stick the quill down with tape.

Quill

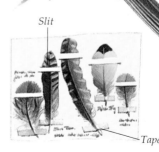

Slit

Tape

9

Towns and cities

In very built up areas of cities, you may see only sparrows, starlings and pigeons. Where there are parks and gardens you will find other species of birds too.

Juvenile

Starlings

| 22cm |

Adult in winter

Starlings are noisy birds which are often seen feeding and roosting in enormous flocks.

Swift

| 17cm |

Very long, curved wings

Sooty black plumage

Short, forked tail

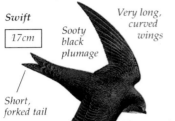

Flocks of Swifts fly very fast over towns, catching insects. They are seen from May until August.

Swallow

| 19cm |

Long, forked tail

Red throat patch

Swallows can be seen catching insects over rivers and reservoirs.

Long, pointed wings

Female hovering

Kestrels

| 34cm |

Kestrels hover when they are hunting. In towns they often eat small birds and make nests at the top of buildings.

Male

House Sparrows

| 15cm |

Female

Male

House Sparrows are familiar small birds that even live in city centres, often in flocks.

Female

Black Redstarts

14cm

Male

Black Redstarts once nested mainly on cliffs, but now also nest in towns. They are rare in Britain.

House Martins build their mud nests under the eaves of houses. They catch insects in flight.

House Martin

12.5cm

Wide white band on throat

Black-headed Gull 37cm

Black-headed Gulls are seen inland as well as near the sea. The head is dark in summer only.

Jackdaw

33cm

Grey on nape

Jackdaws may be found in town parks and near ruins and old buildings.

Canada Geese are large and noisy. They can often be seen on park lakes in towns.

Canada Goose

95cm

Pigeons

Town, or Feral, Pigeons are descended from Rock Doves which nest on sea cliffs. Town Pigeons are often very tame and can be a nuisance. Their plumage varies greatly.

Rock Dove

33cm

Feral Pigeon

33cm

Woodpigeons are larger than Feral Pigeons, but often mix with them. Look for white patches on the neck and wings.

Wood-pigeon 41cm

Woods and forests

The trees, shrubs and undergrowth of woods and forests provide nesting places, food and shelter for many different species.

Jay

32cm

Nuthatches climb up and down trees in a series of short hops. They nest in tree-holes.

Nuthatch 14cm

Jays are secretive woodland birds with harsh, screeching calls.

Look for white rump in flight.

27cm *Nightjar*

Treecreepers climb tree trunks in search of food, then fly down again.

Treecreeper

13cm

Nightjars are seldom seen in daylight. Listen for their non-stop purring calls after dark.

Woodpeckers

Woodpeckers chisel out holes in trees for nesting and drum on trees to mark their territory. Woodpeckers are not found in Ireland.

Great Spotted Woodpecker 23cm

Lesser Spotted Woodpecker

14cm

Stripes on back

Look for large white patches on the wings.

The Lesser Spotted Woodpecker prefers open woods. It is not found in Scotland.

The Great Spotted Woodpecker is the size of a Song Thrush.

Birds in conifer forests

Crossbills nest in pinewoods in parts of Scotland and northern Europe. They break into pine cones to feed on the seeds.

Male

Crossbills

16cm

Female

The beak has crossed tips for splitting the scales of pine cones.

Capercaillies live in pine forests in Scotland and other parts of northern Europe. They eat pine shoots at the tips of branches.

Capercaillies

61cm

Male

Female

Goldcrest

9cm

Female (the male's crest is orange).

The tiny Goldcrest is the smallest bird in Europe. It is often found in pinewoods.

Long-eared Owl

34cm

Long-eared Owls hunt at night and usually nest in conifer forests. Their long "ear" tufts cannot be seen in flight.

Siskins usually nest in conifers. They are often seen in flocks with Redpolls (see page 14).

Female

Siskins

11cm

Male

Crested Tit

11.5cm

Crested Tits are widespread in most of Europe, but in Britain are only found in a few Scottish pinewoods.

13

More woodland birds

Redpolls live in plantations and birch woods. In parts of northern Europe they are paler than in Britain.

Redpolls

12cm

Pied Flycatchers catch insects in the air but also feed on the ground. They are seen in woods in summer.

Pied Flycatchers

13cm

Male *Female*

Coal Tits are active birds. They like conifers, but may be seen in other trees too.

White patch on back of head

Coal Tit

11.5cm

Marsh Tit

Marsh Tits like dry, deciduous woods. They are seldom seen in gardens.

11.5cm

Nightingale

17cm

Nightingales are shy birds which prefer woods with dense undergrowth. They are best found by listening for their song in May and June.

Reddish tail

Redstarts

14cm

Female

Redstarts are seen in woods, parks and other places where there are scattered trees.

Woodcock   34cm

Male

The Woodcock is a secretive bird that lives in damp woods. Watch for its display flight over woods at dusk in early summer.

Long-tailed Tit

14cm

Look for the long tail in flight.

Hedges and the edges of woodlands are good places to see Long-tailed Tits. They move through trees and hedges in small flocks.

Woodland warblers

The Blackcap, a species of warbler, is a common summer visitor to woods. It moves from perch to perch as it sings.

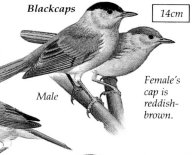

Blackcaps

14cm

Male

Female's cap is reddish-brown.

Garden Warbler

Garden Warblers like woods with thick hedges or undergrowth. They sing from dense cover and are hard to see.

14cm

The Wood Warbler sings from a branch, repeating a note faster and faster until it becomes a trill.

Yellow breast

Wood Warbler

12.5cm

Chiffchaff *Round head*

Dark legs

The Chiffchaff is a species of warbler. Its repetitive "chiff-chaff" song can be heard in woods and from bushes.

Willow Warbler

Flattish head

11cm

Wings longer than Chiffchaff's

The Willow Warbler looks very similar to the Chiffchaff. Its song, which comes down the scale, is the best way to identify it.

Pale legs

11cm

Birds of open country

These are some of the birds you might spot in open countryside such as fields, meadows, marshes, moors, scrub and on heaths and grassland.

Skylarks are often heard singing over farmland. They rise up to a great height, hover, and sail down in full song.

Skylark

18cm

Male

Flicks wings and tail.

Female

Whinchats 13cm

Whinchats perch on top of bushes and posts in open country. Listen for their "tic-tic" calls.

Crested Larks are very rare in Britain but are widespread in central and southern Europe.

17cm

Crested Lark

Meadow Pipits are often seen on moors, but also in fields and other open areas.

Meadow Pipit

14.5cm

Stonechats

13cm

Female

Male

A Stonechat's call sounds like stones knocking together. It is found on heaths, often near the sea.

Wheatears visit moors and barren areas in summer. They are also seen elsewhere in spring and autumn.

Male

Wheatears

15cm

White rump and black tail

Female

Yellowhammers

17cm

Male

Yellowhammers are common in open country, especially farmland. They form flocks in winter.

Linnets

Male

Linnets live on heaths and farmland, but are also found in towns and gardens. They feed on seeds and form flocks in winter.

Female

13cm *Female*

Female

Bramblings

Male's head is brown in winter.

Male

Flocks of Bramblings feed on grain and seeds. They often eat the fruit from beech trees.

Carrion Crow

Hooded Crow

Crows are seen in all kinds of open country. Carrion Crows are seen alone or in pairs. Hooded Crows form flocks.

Rook

46cm

47cm

Rooks are usually seen in flocks, especially on farmland. They nest in "rookeries" at the tops of trees. Their call is a harsh "kaw".

Butcher birds

Shrikes are nicknamed "butcher birds" because they stick their prey on thorns to store it. They swoop down on insects or small animals.

Lizard impaled on thorns by a shrike

Red-backed Shrike

Female

Male

17cm

Great Grey Shrike

24cm

Waterbirds

Areas of water surrounded by trees, bushes and plants are good places to spot a variety of waterbirds.

Mallards are a very widespread species of duck. They feed from the surface of the water and they do not dive.

Mallards

58cm

Female

Male

Pintails 66cm

Female

Male

Pintails use their long necks to feed on plants under the water. Look for them on estuaries and marshes near the sea in winter.

Tufted Ducks are seen on large lakes and reservoirs and also sometimes on town ponds. They dive to find food.

Tufted Ducks 43cm

Female

Male

Female

Male

Teal

35cm

Teal are the smallest European ducks. They are shy birds which prefer the shallow edges of lakes.

Pochards spend much of their time resting on open water and diving for food. They are more likely to be seen in winter.

Pochards *Female* 46cm

Male

Red-breasted Mergansers

Female

58cm

Male

Red-breasted Mergansers breed by lakes and rivers and are often seen near the sea. They are seldom seen inland in winter, but visit coastal areas.

Great Crested Grebes are found on lakes, reservoirs and flooded gravel pits, and on the sea in winter. Pairs of grebes perform elegant dance-like displays during the breeding season.

Summer

Little Grebe *or Dabchick*

27cm

Winter

Summer

Great Crested Grebe

Winter

48cm

Little Grebes, or Dabchicks, are common on inland waters all year, but they are secretive and hard to spot. Their call is a shrill trill.

Coot

Adult has a white shield on forehead.

Coots are usually seen on lakes and reservoirs, rather than ponds. They dive to feed on water plants.

38cm

Moorhen

Red bill with yellow tip

33cm

Moorhens live and breed near ponds, lakes or streams. They are shy birds which bob their heads as they swim.

Waterbird tracks

Look out for the tracks of waterbirds in the mud on riverbanks and around ponds, lakes and puddles.

Web

Claws

Mallard tracks

Moorhen

Coot

Grey Heron

Greylag Goose

More waterbirds

White-fronted Geese nest in the Arctic and fly south for the winter. Look for white at the base of the bill.

Brent Goose | 58cm

Thin white band

White-fronted Goose | 71cm

Brent Geese are the same size as Mallards. Look out for them on estuaries in winter.

Pink-footed Geese feed on arable land. They are seen in winter in Scotland and coastal areas of England.

Bean Goose

| 80cm

Orange legs

Look for pink legs.

Pink-footed Goose | 68cm

Bean Geese are rare winter visitors from northern Europe. They graze on inland pastures or fields of young corn.

Some Greylag Geese breed in Britain, but many arrive just for the winter.

Barnacle Geese are seen on the west coasts of Britain and Ireland in winter and sometimes in parks.

Greylag Goose | 82cm

| 63cm **Barnacle Goose**

Mute Swan

| 152cm

Mute Swans are often seen on lakes and rivers. Adults have an orange bill with a black lump on it.

Specialist feeders

Many waterbirds have specially shaped beaks and bodies which help them to find food in a particular way.

Kingfishers have long beaks and short tails. They fly fast over the water and dive into it to catch fish.

Dagger-shaped beaks

Grey Heron

92cm

17cm

Kingfisher

Grey Herons use their long beaks to catch fish, frogs and small mammals. They have long legs for wading.

The long legs stick out in flight.

Grey Wagtail

18cm

Wags tail up and down

Male in summer

Grey Wagtails live near fast-flowing streams and catch insects in flight.

Shovelers like quiet lakes and shallow water. They use their long bills to filter food from the water.

Female

Shovelers

51cm

Male

Diving dippers

Dippers live near fast-flowing water. They run down rocks or dive into the water with their eyes open.

Under the water, they walk along the bed of the stream, looking for insects and snails to eat.

When they have caught something, they hop out of the water and stand on a rock to eat it.

Seabirds

In summer, cliffs and seashores are good places to spot birds. Many species which spend the rest of the year out at sea come ashore for the breeding season to lay their eggs. Some nest together in enormous groups called colonies.

Puffins have very colourful bills in the breeding season.

Puffin

30cm

Puffins nest in burrows which they dig out near the tops of cliffs. Kittiwakes make nests on ledges. Guillemots lay eggs on bare ledges and Razorbills lay eggs on ledges under overhanging rocks.

Reddish feet in summer

— **Kittiwake**

Look for black wing tips in flight.

Gannet

92cm

Gannets dive head-first into the sea to catch fish. They form huge colonies of up to 20,000 birds.

— **Guillemot**

Herring Gulls are widespread and noisy. They are very often seen inland as well as near the sea.

Herring Gulls are larger than Common Gulls.

Razorbill

56cm

Herring Gull

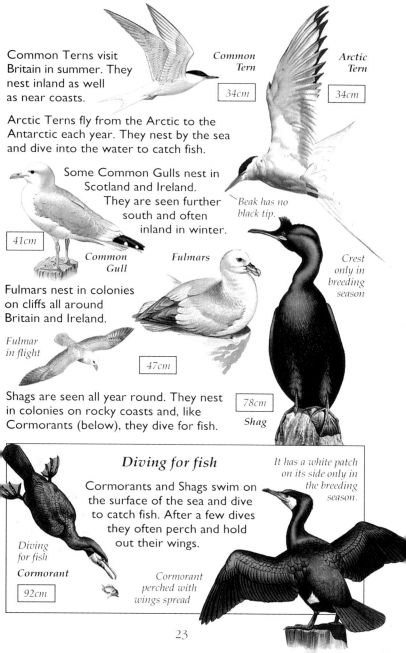

Common Terns visit Britain in summer. They nest inland as well as near coasts.

Common Tern

34cm

Arctic Tern

34cm

Arctic Terns fly from the Arctic to the Antarctic each year. They nest by the sea and dive into the water to catch fish.

Some Common Gulls nest in Scotland and Ireland. They are seen further south and often inland in winter.

Beak has no black tip.

41cm

Common Gull

Fulmars

Crest only in breeding season

Fulmars nest in colonies on cliffs all around Britain and Ireland.

Fulmar in flight

47cm

Shags are seen all year round. They nest in colonies on rocky coasts and, like Cormorants (below), they dive for fish.

78cm

Shag

Diving for fish

Cormorants and Shags swim on the surface of the sea and dive to catch fish. After a few dives they often perch and hold out their wings.

It has a white patch on its side only in the breeding season.

Diving for fish

Cormorant

92cm

Cormorant perched with wings spread

23

Seashores and estuaries

Seashores, salt marshes and estuaries (tidal mouths of rivers) are great places to spot birds. Many species come to feed there.

Shelduck

61cm

Shelducks feed on small shellfish in shallow water. They often nest in rabbit holes.

Male

Bar-tailed Godwits are mostly seen in spring and autumn. Some winter on estuaries in Britain and Ireland.

38cm

Bar-tailed Godwit

Dunlins are common visitors to shores, but they nest on moors.

Winter

Dunlin

19cm

Summer

At low tide, many species of birds search for food together.

Oystercatchers use their bills to open shellfish.

Avocets filter tiny animals from the water with long, curved bills.

Turnstones move stones to find crabs and sandhoppers.

43cm *Oystercatcher*   *Avocet* 43cm   *Turnstone* 23cm

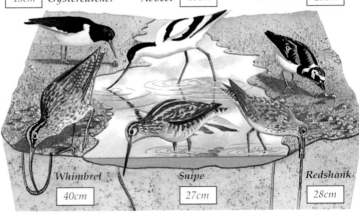

Whimbrel
40cm

Snipe
27cm

Redshank
28cm

Whimbrels probe deeply for worms and other animals.

Snipe open the tips of their bills under the ground to grab worms.

Redshanks look for worms and shellfish in the mud or sand.

Sanderling
20cm

Summer

Sanderlings run along the water's edge on sandy shores, looking for small sea creatures washed up by the waves.

Ringed Plovers are seen on sandy and shingle shores, and on estuaries in winter. Many nest on shingle beaches.

Ringed Plovers
19cm

Juvenile

Summer

A Plover's markings break up its outline so it is hard to spot against its background.

A few Black-tailed Godwits nest in Britain, but they are more often seen on coasts during the winter months.

41cm

Black-tailed Godwits

Knots are seen in large flocks in winter. They like sand or mudflats in estuaries.

Knot
25cm

Winter

Greenshanks are rarer and larger than Redshanks (see page 24). They are seen in spring and autumn on coasts or inland. Some nest in northern Scotland.

Greenshank
30cm

Look for its long, green legs.

Curlew
48–64cm

Bill similar to Whimbrel's (see page 24) but longer.

Whitish belly

The Curlew is the largest European shorebird. It breeds on moors and bogs but is seen on coasts at other times of the year.

Curlew tracks

25

Birds of prey

Birds of prey have sharp, hooked bills and curved claws. They hunt other animals. There are two main groups: owls (see page 28) and raptors. The raptors include buzzards hawks, falcons, eagles, kites, harriers and vultures.

Sparrowhawk
Female

38cm

Broad, rounded wings with slight "fingers"

Birds of prey have sharp eyes for spotting prey and hooked bills for tearing flesh.

Sparrowhawks hunt birds along woodland edges and hedges. The female is browner and slightly larger than the male.

Long legs for grasping prey

Sharp talons (claws)

Very long, flexible tail aids steering

Ospreys are rare summer visitors to Britain. They swoop down on fish and snatch them up in their talons.

58cm *Osprey*

Honey Buzzards are rare summer visitors to British woodlands. They eat mainly grubs and wasps.

Soars with wings held flat

Grey head

Honey Buzzards

51-59cm

Buzzards are often seen soaring over farmland and moors as they hunt.

Buzzard

54cm

Neck and tail longer than Buzzard's

26

Juvenile

Golden Eagles

Golden Eagles can glide long distances. They live in the Scottish Highlands. Juveniles have white on the wings and tail.

Goshawks live in dense woodlands. The male is smaller than the female. They are rare in Britain.

Very long, broad wings

Adult

83cm

Peregrine striking Rock Dove

Goshawk
Male

48cm

Goshawk
Female

58cm

Peregrine

38-48cm

Red Kites

62cm

Peregrines dive at speed on flying birds. They are seen near cliffs and inland crags and hunting over estuaries and marshes in winter.

The Hobby is a small falcon with long wings and a short tail. It hunts prey in the air and may feed in flight.

Red Kites can soar for long periods. They are rare in Britain.

Hobby feeding on the wing

Hobbies

33cm

Owls

Most species of owl hunt after sunset. Their excellent eyesight and hearing allow them to pinpoint prey even in dim light. All owls have very flexible necks and can turn their heads almost right around.

Tawny Owls

38cm

Tawny Owls call with a familiar "hoot". They hunt at night where there are woods or old trees.

—— *Tawny Owl returning to its nest with a vole*

Little Owl

22cm

Little Owls hunt at dusk, flying low over farmland and open country. They nest in tree-holes and eat many insects in summer. When curious, they bob up and down.

Barn Owls often nest in hollow trees or old buildings. They hunt small birds and mammals and call with an eerie shriek.

Short-eared Owls hunt voles and other small mammals in daylight as well as at dusk.

Short-eared Owl

37cm

Barn Owls

34cm

In northern and eastern Europe, Barn Owls have darker faces and breasts.

Gamebirds

Gamebirds have plump, round bodies and small chicken-like heads. They may be hard to see, but if disturbed, they rise up into the air with a sudden noise.

Pheasants
Female

58cm

Pheasants live on farmland with hedges and nest on the ground. They are often reared for shooting.

Very long tail

Male

87cm

Ptarmigan

34cm

Winter

Ptarmigan live on barren mountain tops in Scotland. They blend in with the background. (See also page 5.)

Black Grouse

Male 53cm

41cm

Female

Partridges are often found in small groups. They like farmland with hedges. Their call is a rather grating "kirr-ic".

30cm *Partridge*

Black Grouse are often found on the edge of moorland, sometimes perched in trees, or eating buds.

Red Grouse live on moors in Britain and Ireland. They are seen all the year round.

Red-legged Partridge

34cm

Red Grouse

Male 36cm

Female

Red-legged Partridges are often seen in fields and open sandy areas.

Scorecard

All the birds shown in this book are listed here, in alphabetical order. When you spot one, fill in the date next to its name. You can add up your score after a day out birdwatching.

	Score	Date seen
Arctic Tern	15	
Avocet	25	
Barnacle Goose	20	
Barn Owl	15	
Bar-tailed Godwit	20	
Bean Goose	25	
Blackbird	5	
Blackcap	10	
Black Grouse	15	
Black-headed Gull	5	
Black Redstart	20	
Black-tailed Godwit	20	
Blue Tit	5	
Brambling	15	
Brent Goose	15	
Bullfinch	10	
Buzzard	15	
Canada Goose	5	
Capercaillie	20	
Carrion Crow	5	
Chaffinch	5	
Chiffchaff	10	
Coal Tit	10	
Collared Dove	5	
Common Gull	15	
Common Tern	10	
Coot	5	
Cormorant	10	
Crested Lark	25	
Crested Tit	25	
Crossbill	20	
Cuckoo	10	
Curlew	10	
Dipper	15	

	Score	Date seen
Dunlin	10	
Dunnock	5	
Feral Pigeon	5	
Fieldfare	10	
Fulmar	10	
Gannet	15	
Garden Warbler	15	
Goldcrest	10	
Golden Eagle	25	
Goldfinch	10	
Goshawk	25	
Great Crested Grebe	10	
Great Grey Shrike	25	
Great Spotted Woodpecker	10	
Great Tit	5	
Greenfinch	10	
Greenshank	20	
Green Woodpecker	15	
Grey Heron	10	
Greylag Goose	10	
Grey Wagtail	10	
Guillemot	15	
Herring Gull	5	
Hobby	20	
Honey Buzzard	25	
Hooded Crow	15	
House Martin	10	
House Sparrow	5	
Jackdaw	10	
Jay	10	
Kestrel	10	
Kingfisher	15	
Kittiwake	15	
Knot	15	

	Score	Date seen
Lesser Spotted Woodpecker	20	
Linnet	10	
Little Grebe	15	
Little Owl	15	
Long-eared Owl	20	
Long-tailed Tit	10	
Magpie	5	
Mallard	5	
Marsh Tit	15	
Meadow Pipit	15	
Mistle Thrush	10	
Moorhen	5	
Mute Swan	5	
Nightingale	15	
Nightjar	15	
Nuthatch	15	
Osprey	25	
Oystercatcher	10	
Partridge	15	
Peregrine	20	
Pheasant	5	
Pied Flycatcher	15	
Pied Wagtail	10	
Pink-footed Goose	15	
Pintail	15	
Pochard	10	
Ptarmigan	20	
Puffin	20	
Razorbill	15	
Red-backed Shrike	25	
Red-breasted Merganser	20	
Red Grouse	15	
Red Kite	20	
Red-legged Partridge	15	
Redpoll	15	
Redshank	10	

	Score	Date seen
Redstart	15	
Redwing	10	
Ringed Plover	15	
Robin	5	
Rock Dove	25	
Rook	10	
Sanderling	15	
Shag	15	
Shelduck	15	
Short-eared Owl	20	
Shoveler	15	
Siskin	15	
Skylark	10	
Snipe	15	
Song Thrush	5	
Sparrowhawk	15	
Spotted Flycatcher	10	
Starling	5	
Stonechat	15	
Swallow	10	
Swift	10	
Tawny Owl	15	
Teal	15	
Tengmalm's Owl	25	
Treecreeper	15	
Tufted Duck	10	
Turnstone	15	
Wheatear	15	
Whimbrel	20	
Whinchat	15	
White-fronted Goose	20	
White Wagtail	25	
Willow Warbler	10	
Woodcock	15	
Woodpigeon	5	
Wood Warbler	15	
Wren	5	
Yellowhammer	10	

Index

Additional illustrations: Alan Harris, Tim Hayward, Maurice Pledger, Ian Wallace, David Wright.

This book is based on material previously published in *The Usborne Spotter's Guides to Birds, Town and City Wildlife, Birds of Prey* and *Sea and Freshwater Birds, Usborne Science and Nature: Ornithology, Usborne Guide to Birds of Britain and Europe, The Usborne Nature Trail Books of Birdwatching* and *Garden Wildlife, The Usborne Book of World Wildlife.*

First published in 1996 by Usborne Publishing Ltd, Usborne House, 83-85 Saffron Hill, London EC1 8RT, England.